PORTALS
A Year of Meditation

Ann Higgins
Devi Padmini Krishnananda

PORTALS
A Year of Meditation

Ann Higgins

Copyright © 2014 by Barbara Ann Higgins
Published 2015
All rights reserved

ISBN: 978-0-692-29208-2

Cover design by Dan Boone

Mountain Lotus Publishing
Ann@yogaportals.com
Flagstaff, Arizona

INVOCATION

I have chanted this mantra for many years as part of my morning *sadhana* (practice) and always at the beginning of my Tuesday night yoga class. It is a fitting beginning for this book. This ritual mantra calls on the source of innermost consciousness to provide protection and inspiration from which to bring these writings to life.

The Gayatri Mantra

Om
Bhur bhuvar svah
Tat savitri varenyam
Bhargo divasya demaye
Diyoyo nah prachodayot
Om
Shanti Shanti Shanti

PORTAL: A doorway, gate, or entrance, especially a large and imposing one. Any entrance, often figurative as the Portal of Wisdom.

— *Webster's Dictionary*

DISCLAIMER

Portals meditations are meant to be a spiritual practice. There are benefits that can be derived from practicing meditation, but they should never take the place of medical treatment for physical, mental and emotional problems.

There are many meditations to choose from. If any of them cause discomfort physically, mentally or emotionally, discontinue that practice.

ACKNOWLEDGMENTS

I am happy to acknowledge members of my family and friends who contributed to the making of this book:

Gurani Anjali, my spiritual guide, who made all things possible
Dan Boone, my husband who always encourages me
Norma Kaladas, sister and friend, advisor
Sarita Southgate, friend and advisor
Louella Holter, friend, yoga devotee, and editor

I would also like to thank my family for supporting my lifestyle, and the disciples of Gurani Anjali at Yoga Anand Ashram with whom I shared the privilege of close relationship for many years. I would also like to say thank you to all of my students over the last 40 years; without you I would not have had the opportunity to give back what I have been blessed to have received. Finally, my thanks go to all those who encouraged me to write this book.

CONTENTS

Introduction
How to Use this Book
About Yoga Lessons
Basic Instructions for Practice
Namaste
The Portals
  1. Clear and Refresh
  2. Attention without Tension
  3. Freedom from Action
  4. Inner Environment
  5. Listen
  6. Haiku
  7. The Flower
  8. Colors
  9. Be An Island Unto Yourself
  10. Do All in the Presence of Love
  11. Your Real Mother and Father
  12. The Blanket of Peace
  13. Your Personal Rhythm
  14. Pratyahara
  15. Poised
  16. Forgiveness
  17. A Healing Bath
  18. Be Breathed
  19. Om
  20. The End of the Sentence
  21. A Mini-Vacation
  22. Soham
  23. The Lake of the Mind
  24. Holding an Orange

25. Explore Yourself
26. Peace Mantra
27. Vishuddha Chakra
28. Path to the Heart of Love
29. Aparigraha
30. Listen Without Naming
31. Something Perfect Exists
32. Breathe
33. Day of the Dead Celebration
34. Smile
35. Freedom from Thinking
36. Be an Artist
37. Assertiveness and Aggression
38. Winter Solstice Healing Meditation
39. Unfocused Awareness
40. Anahata
41. Still Point
42. Overcoming Unhappiness
43. Cloudless Sky
44. Cross Breathing
45. Transfixed
46. One With All
47. Fear and Depression
48. Windows of the Soul
49. Wake Up And Celebrate
50. Sing this Song
51. Sitting
52. Guru Purnima

INTRODUCTION AND BIOGRAPHY

In 1968 my life was not going as planned. I had recently divorced, was caring for a teenage niece, was unemployed, and was questioning all the reasons that had brought me to this point and deciding what my next chapter would be.

I was studying yoga mostly through books, including *The Autobiography of a Yogi* by Paramahansa Yogananda, and had been subscribing to yoga lessons for about a year through his Self-Realization Center. I decided to take a break and visit the center in Hollywood, California. While there, walking the beautiful grounds, I had an amazing experience of all-inclusiveness that convinced me that yoga was the right path. I came home feeling at peace with myself and knowing that the past was over and I was going to move on. I became even more convinced that yoga was a way of life that could help me.

I moved back into the family home. An old friend who lived nearby called to say that a woman from India was teaching yoga in her area and did I want to go to her class. Arriving in class, I was greeted by a small Indian woman in a sari with the most beautiful smile you can imagine. I couldn't believe my luck in finding a teacher. Even at this first class I felt drawn to her. She seemed to exude love. I would find that to be true and it was a magnetic force that would draw me to her forever.

I stayed with Gurani Anjali (also called Guruma) for the next thirteen years. I became her personal secretary, the assistant director of the Ashram, and her friend. During the first few years I was studying with the Gurani and teaching yoga in schools, libraries, and anywhere we could gather a group of students. A small group of devotees gathered at her house. The group was male and female, a mix of housewives, hippies, and people college age to middle age. My life revolved around this community of students living the yoga way of life. This meant following a system called Ashtanga yoga, an eight-step system of purification, psychology, and philosophy. Accordingly, we fasted, kept silence, and did yoga postures, breathing techniques, and meditation every day. We lived the principle of nonviolence.

We learned to wear saris, sit cross-legged on the floor, and cook Indian food as we discussed the yoga philosophy and hung on every word our Gurani said. She talked of her vision to start an Ashram, something we knew nothing about. It was in 1972 that we acquired our own space and became a non-profit organization. Some of her devotees became what she called Pillars and we dedicated our lives to continuing to teach yoga, and running the organization. At various times over the years this included classes in beginning and advanced yoga, meditation every Sunday morning, monthly membership meetings, and celebration of many festivals serving vegetarian dinners. We opened a restaurant called Santosha, an art gallery, a tailoring shop, and a bookstore.

We also invited guest lecturers and swamis to speak and musicians for concerts.

It was also a time when my spiritual development matured into another realization of the unity of all life. Guruma conducted a ritual and said I was in *Samadhi*. After following a set of instructions that included three days of fasting, purification, and meditation, I was given a personal mantra and the formal name of Devi Padmini Krishnananda.

Many years later I left the Ashram community and moved to another state. I kept in touch with Guruma by telephone and visited every couple of years. She passed away in 2001. I continued to dedicate myself to teaching yoga until 2010, having two or three classes per week and giving workshops and lectures. Gurani Anjali told me to "write it down," and that is how I am now teaching. I hope my love of yoga and meditation comes through these portals, bringing wisdom and love to all who read them.

HOW TO USE THIS BOOK

This book presents 52 meditations that can be approached in various ways. My hope is that you will use them over and over for many years to come. As they become more familiar to you, you will know better how you want to use the book. I suggest that you read through all of them initially to get a feeling for the direction the book is taking you. You will find that some will feel just right to you from the first reading, while others may take a few readings before being fully understood. After the initial reading go back to the first one, "Clear and Refresh." It is an easy and immediately effective meditation. Read it a couple of times. As you sink into your breathing, you will begin to experience the meditation. You are there; simply stay and enjoy the time.

As you will see, each one is a different story. Some are brief and immediate, and others require more reading and contemplation. I have tried to arrange the portals so that you can make a choice depending on what is needed at any given time. For example, after your initial reading of the entire selection from 1 to 52, start at the beginning and work with Portal 1 for a week. The following week, chose Portal 2 and so on. By selecting one at a time and doing it for 7 days you will be fully involved in understanding, experimentation, and realization. Each one is an experiment; it will bring you to a different realization each time you sit.

When you begin, follow the portal just as it is written. In time, your meditation will become a very personal experience, opening up your subconscious for you to examine and experience. Pay attention to where it takes you. Some portals are very personal. They follow my own experience, my thinking as I fall into a meditative state; many are similar to poetry.

Some of the portals are more about lessons in how we think—how much negative thinking we are engaged in and how to go about turning harmful and hurtful negative thoughts into healthy, productive, and positive ones. Others investigate an idea that can bring us to another level of consciousness. There will be times when you will not initially comprehend an idea, and then slowly as you work with it, you will find yourself understanding more and more. You will be following tracks I have laid down based on my own personal experience. Each time you sit to use the book, you will have the opportunity to learn, to enjoy, and to grow.

ABOUT YOGA LESSONS

I have included a section called Yoga Lesson with some of the portals to provide additional information regarding the science-philosophy of yoga where I felt it would be helpful or interesting for the reader. An excellent book for Sanskrit translations is Georg Feuerstein's book *The Encyclopedic Dictionary of Yoga*.

Much of my yoga training with Gurani Anjali was taken from *The Yoga Sutras of Patanjali*. Book Two, *Sadhana Pada 29*, lists the eight limbs of Yoga. The first five are (1) *Yama* (abstinence), (2) *Niyama* (observance), (3) *Asana* (posture), (4) *Pranayama* (breath control), and (5) *Pratyahara* (sense withdrawal). The last three are (6) *Dharana* (concentration), (7) *Dhyana* (meditation), and (8) *Samadhi* (absorption). In *Portals* we will concentrate on the last three steps, although you will find that the other steps have a place here as well.

The process begins with the third step, *asana* (posture), taking a firm seat and applying a breathing technique (*pranayama*). You have made your decision to bring your mind and attention to the chosen portal. You are now fully engaged physically, mentally and emotionally. This stage of detachment and withdrawal is called *pratyahara*, and it is the fifth step in the system. You have gathered your senses and like a tortoise drawing in its head and limbs, you close the door to the world of sense perception. You are ready for the inward journey.

The last three steps are like ancient guides holding open the portal for you to enter. Concentration (*dharana*) deepens as attention is brought to an energy center such as the heart center or *ajna* center. (The portal you've chosen will instruct you.) Now that you have made the decision and are holding to one thought, consciousness rises to the next level, which is meditation (*dhyana*). Notice how that first decision to sit and pay attention guides you to the next. Taking your time to concentrate, and holding to that intention, you are rewarded with a stronger penetration of the subject, and an opening of the door to the source of consciousness.

The final, eighth step (*samadhi*) of Patanjali's yoga system has been translated in various ways—spiritual absorption is one, enstasy from the *Encyclopedic Dictionary of Yoga* and others simply say "bliss." There are also various types and levels of the experience that can be explored by reading the texts I, 41.

As practitioners we can only participate in the process up to this point. If you continue to hold this one thought, you may experience *samadhi* and go beyond the ego. I advise you not to dwell on the result of the meditation; it is the process itself that leads to a result that we often cannot measure.

You do not need to know yoga to practice the portals, but keep in mind that the eight steps do not necessarily follow a linear sequence of 1 through 8, like climbing stairs. Practicing the portals will help you to develop the ability to concentrate and to hold to one point. If you wish to meditate, this one-pointedness is a most important first step. It is *citta vrittri nirodha*, the "modification of thought waves in the mind" that will bring the yogi to the state of bliss.

BASIC INSTRUCTIONS FOR PRACTICE

Find a place that is clean and safe. If you decide to sit outside, keep in mind that there are many distractions, and that may not be the best choice for doing some of the meditations. Having said that, there are indeed beautiful places outdoors to sit and meditate. If you find yourself in such a setting and it is conducive to meditation, by all means go for it.

Make sure you will not be disturbed. Turn off your telephone and cell phone. Ask your family to give you a half hour to meditate. Small children and pets do not understand and will probably climb on your lap; they are drawn to the peace and quiet. It is wonderful to allow this to happen occasionally for a few minutes. You will be gently introducing the child to quiet time in this otherwise busy life. However, if they are disruptive and you want to be alone, you'll need to plan ahead with your family. Pets may be better left out of the room.

You may sit on the floor, but sitting on a chair is more comfortable for most people. Use a chair with a straight, comfortable back. Always begin by reminding yourself that you are going to devote a set amount of time for each portal. If you have time constraints, or want to discipline yourself to a certain amount of time, then set a timer just far enough away so you can still hear it. Allow about 15 minutes. You may later find that you want to take more time; it really depends on you. Keep in mind that you do not want to force yourself to meditate. It should be a pleasant experience that you look forward to. So be kind. If you sit and just read a portal for a few minutes, and then extend the time each time you sit, before you know it you will have enjoyed a very pleasant 15 to 30 minutes.

The time of day when you practice is a personal choice, but morning has always been a wonderful time for me. I love to get up early before there's a lot of activity. Dawn and dusk have long been considered ideal times for meditation, when there's a natural stillness that is very conducive to meditation. Try it.

You might ask, why would I meditate? Many answers might come—for peace of mind, to treat high blood pressure, to feel joy and happiness, to reach nirvana, to feel bliss—and they can all be realized.

THE PORTALS

Namaste

Namaste is a respectful greeting that means "I bow to you." It is usually combined with a gesture of placing the hands together at chest level in line with your heart in a posture called Anjali (which also happens to be my Gurani's name) to acknowledge the divine spirit within. It is a respectful greeting in India, much like shaking hands but with more meaning. I learned it from my Gurani the very first day of yoga class, when it was done at the beginning and end of each of her classes. For many years in the Ashram we would also greet each other in this manner whenever we met. To greet our Gurani in a more respectful and devotional way our hands would be folded in Anjali and then touch the third eye center at the forehead and then down to the heart chakra center while bowing the head. It is also a way to release the power of ego dominance for a few seconds.

My students often asked me to come home with them, and that is why I wrote portals. In order to better connect with me, and my intention in writing *Portals*, fold your hands in Anjali and be with me in spirit. *Namaste*.

Portal 1
CLEAR AND REFRESH

This is a very simple and effective exercise. A friend has described it as her "go to place," whenever she feels bogged down. It takes just a few minutes to clear the mind and feel refreshed, and it can be done almost anywhere. Speaking of anywhere, I recently had lunch with a friend who was also my yoga student for several years. She is a wonderful woman who recently signed up to travel to Haiti with a group of medically trained personnel. She is a physical therapist and Tai Yoga instructor. The first time she was there she brought this portal and three others with her and read them to several other workers when they were able to take a break from work. She said they were a gift of calm in the midst of chaos and the group was very appreciative.

Practice
Begin with a few deep and relaxing breaths:
Breathe out and *clear* the mind
Breathe in and *refresh* the mind
Rest in the breath at the junction of the inhaled and exhaled breath
Breathe in rest breathe out rest
Keep the mind perfectly centered
The body perfectly still
Here and now

Keep your attention here and now
Breathe and center yourself between the inner and outer worlds
Where the in breath meets the out breath
Where the out breath meets the in breath
Stay at that point with no tension
With joy in the moment of pure awareness.

Portal 2
ATTENTION WITHOUT TENSION

Today we'll pay close attention to what is right here in front of us, regardless of whether we deem it important or not. This exercise releases us from extra effort.

An example from my own experience goes back to the beginning of my personal relationship with Gurani Anjali. I was invited to come to her home one afternoon. When I arrived, she was sorting laundry; when you went to her home you participated in whatever work was going on. I picked up the towels and began to fold and stack. I worked fast and furiously to get it done, just as I had done at my own home. She started to smile and then to laugh: "Are you trying to kill the towels?"

I was puzzled, what was wrong? I was really gaining on this pile of laundry. I felt another lesson coming. I was wasting energy and not having a good time. I was beating up the towels and myself as my body tensed with purpose, and my mind was focused on completing the task. Definitely not in the now. I learned something that day and you can be sure that now every time I fold towels, I smile.

Notice the way you work. Are you thinking about the result, or are you in the moment with whatever you are doing? The Sages tell us over and over to "be in the moment," but most of us are far behind it, or way ahead. See if you can be aware of whatever you are doing and stay with it. Perform every act with attention and intention, and don't be in a hurry to get it done. Each moment is precious and life takes place in the here and now, not in the past or the future.

Practice

Today make it a habit to slow down. Whatever chore you have to do today, try to really experience what you are doing. It doesn't matter how important you think the particular job is, or how menial, just be with it—slow down. If the telephone rings or you get a text, don't feel that you need to rush into a response (unless it is an emergency). Take your own time and when you do the work or answer the call, give it all you've got. Give it your full attention.

Portal 3
FREEDOM FROM ACTION

There are times when we just have to give ourselves a break. We need to release ourselves from the overload of thinking and acting. Just reading this portal can give you instant relief from stress. It doesn't say stop everything; it says suspend and hold back. It tells you this is temporary. You'll get back to whatever it is you were doing. It isn't demanding. At times when a hard decision has to be made, and you feel overwhelmed, it can be helpful to hold back and re-center yourself. I've heard that it is wise to wait three days before making an important decision. Here we take just a few minutes, or as much time as you need.

Practice
Start with a few deep, relaxing breaths and read the following more than once if needed.

Suspend action
Suspend thinking
Suspend reaching out
Suspend taking in
Suspend all thoughts
Let the thoughts float in suspension
Let the action be contained in the breath
Until there is only breathing

and suspension
Balance at the center of suspension
Suspend sense activity
Suspend the eyes from looking
the nose from smelling
the ears from hearing
the skin from touching
Suspend and remain in the center of suspension
Hold back from action
As you gently nourish your emptiness with the fullness of emptiness.

Now sit in the suspension until you feel ready to resume activity.

Portal 4
INNER ENVIRONMENT

Just as we fix up our own home in a way that pleases us, the same is possible with our inner environment. Thoughts fill our mind and often dictate how we feel and what actions we will take. Know that it is possible to change negative thinking and instead create a place that you love to come home to.

Even though we do not like being in a room with someone who is always looking at the dark side, we will spend many days of our lives living up-close and personal with negative thoughts dominating our own mind. We chew on old hurts. We reenact battles and conversations. Drama after drama unfolds. My Gurani would say it was like watching a Grade B movie. Negative thinking can be changed. You cannot change another, but you can change yourself. You know it feels so much better to live with calmness and love. Recognizing that you have the ability to change your emotions is the starting point.

You may not always have immediate results, but if you repeat this practice, the negative power will eventually give up. Once you are aware of your ability to change these feelings, it will get easier and the time it takes to change the emotion will shorten.

Practice

The first thing to do is cultivate the desire to change your attitude. You have to *want* to rid yourself of the negative thinking. Begin by finding a place to sit without distraction. We will use a sweeping breath to chase away the accumulating negative energy. Some people like to add a physical movement to the exercise. Create your own or try the following: Exhale and push your hands out, getting rid of the anger. As you inhale pull in and feel the clean new breath.

Negative thinking depletes our energy. Positive energy is invigorating. With each deep breath you take, exhale the dark, negative energy just as you would sweep up the dirt and filth on the floor and throw it out. When you inhale take in clear, clean *prana*, the breath of life. See these positive thoughts as sparkling light energy. Imagine your negative thoughts as dirt on the floor, dark and stinky. As you sweep it up and breathe it out you will begin to feel much lighter, and in control of your emotions.

Keep breathing deeply and slowly until you feel the negative emotion losing its power. Inhale fresh clean restorative energy. Exhale with the sweeping breath. Gather up all of the black toxic negative energy that is holding you back. Inhale the present moment. Exhale the past. Continue the sweeping breath for as long as you are still feeling bogged down. Your inner space is getting more beautiful with each breath.

When you are finished gently return to your baseline breath (normal breathing pattern) and place your hands on your heart center and say, I am at peace. I wish peace to all beings on this planet.

There is great value in learning this portal. First, you now have a technique for releasing negative thinking, and once you have experienced the result, you can use it anytime. Second, you will no longer hold on to negative emotions for very long because you have proven to yourself how easily they can be changed. I have noticed, however, that there are times when we really want to indulge ourselves in a negative emotion. (Like watching that Grade B movie.) We get caught up in it and just won't let it go, even when it is bad. It is not that we can't, we don't want to. You decide.

YOGA LESSON: *Samskara* is a Sanskrit word meaning an impression left from a prior thought or action. These *samskaras* are composed of everything we have experienced in our entire life, consciously or unconsciously. Most of our actions and behaviors are based on these past impressions.

My teacher spoke of *samskaras* as seeds that need to be burned in order for them not to continue to produce. The eighth step in the yoga system, *samadhi*, is ultimately the experience that burns these seeds. This breaking of the connection to the past conditioning allows for freedom in the present.

We can weaken these negative tendencies by recognizing that our reaction to being hurt has always been to become angry. Instead, we can really examine why we are angry, and know that we can change past tendencies.

Portal 5
LISTEN

This is a lovely portal that will bring you, as you read it, to a wonderful state of peace and quiet. As you read each line pay attention to the directions and feel it. Once you learn the practice you will find it can be used anytime you have the desire for liberation of inner chatter.

Instead of talking to yourself
Listen to yourself
Listen and pay attention to yourself just as you do when listening to the birds outside your window, or the gentle rain falling on the roof
Listen and be very quiet
Listen without wanting anything
Without grabbing, needing, wanting to know
With innocence listen very quietly to yourself
Do you hear the silence of yourself?
The endless stream of pure sound without words imposed upon it
Listen with keen alertness and no intent.

Portal 6
HAIKU

Take a break from being involved. Let go of the idea that there is someone witnessing. Let go of the observer. There is no one there. This exercise allows you to be totally involved in the experience.

When we are hit suddenly with this concept, it can feel scary. Keep in mind that all is well and nothing has changed.

When a haiku is written, often there is no personal pronoun. It is about the experience. No need for "I" or "you." It just is. Matsuo Basho is one of the master poets. This is an example of writing a haiku without a personal pronoun.

> A solitary
> crow on a bare branch –
> autumn evening

We usually want to comment on everything from a personal viewpoint. Now when you take away the observer, the experience can be appreciated just as it is. Read the example and write a haiku. Notice how difficult it can be to write without a personal pronoun.

Practice

For the rest of the week, see if you can avoid the use of personal pronouns in your everyday speech. This is an exercise we did for *sadhana* when I was in yoga training. By purposely avoiding the "I" we also stop ourselves from telling a personal history or talking about our past—just another way to be in the present moment. Write as many haikus as you can this week.

Portal 7
THE FLOWER

We've all seen beautiful flower gardens and smelled the perfumes of individual flowers. We'll take this to heart and create our personal flower. Perhaps you can recall a particular one that you especially like.

Practice

Place your hands in your lap with the right hand on top of the left. Take a few deep breaths and begin to visualize a flower of your choice. Take your time creating the flower in as much detail as possible. The more detail, the more powerful your concentration will be. Paint it with your mind. What color is it? How big is it? What does it smell like? Now, imagine you are holding the flower in the palm of your hand with its glowing color and sweet scent. As you continue to breathe, use your exhaled breath to release any thoughts other than the flower you've created. Be totally with it, giving it your full attention and love.

This is a simple exercise to increase your ability to slow down and develop powers of concentration. Remember to keep bringing your attention back to your choice of objects.

Portal 8
COLORS

There are colors all around us and we love the colors of blue sky, green grass and trees, the color of our child's eyes, my mother's sparkling blue eyes, your friend's deep green jewel-like eyes. Can we imagine that our emotions have a color? What color do you suppose your happiness is? What color is anger? Do you see a color?

Let us see the colors that I see, just for now, and then perhaps you can choose your own colors. Traditionally, red is seen as anger, the color of fire, the color that really draws our attention. Restaurants color their walls red to keep the crowd "up" and moving, so that they can seat many people in a night. Red is vibrant and rich. It is the color of blood, and passion.

What is the opposite emotion of red? We'll give it a color ID also. Shall we say calmness, peacefulness, and benevolence. What color is that feeling? Move through the spectrum of colors with me and see if we can make a match. Blue, green, white? Blue is calming, pink and yellow are happy colors. White is neutral. Is calmness a neutral feeling? I want to choose blue. The blue of the sky. The expansiveness of blue in the sky. Blue comforts me. It doesn't arouse me.

Practice

Today we'll work with just two emotions, the one of anger and the other of calmness and peacefulness. Using my choices of red for anger and blue for calmness, begin by focusing on your breath. Breathing rather rapidly, begin to imagine that you are fueling the fire of excitement with lots of energy. See how the breath excites and energizes. There is a place for this kind of energy, but imagine this same energetic movement being fired by the emotion of anger, and you feel like you could blast someone out, verbally or physically. Really feel the emotion of excitement and get to know it really well. It is said that anger or *krodha* causes confusion and loss of wisdom.

Now try to change this excitement into calmness. We chose blue for calmness and peacefulness. Breathe slowly and notice that as each breath is taken in and released your mood begins to change. Continue the rhythm and now add the color blue, add the blue sky to your breath and just as water extinguishes fire, cover the red with blue and watch the colors come together, softening the color red. Notice too, how the breath and your intention release your mood from anger to peacefulness without harshness, and without repressing the anger. It is there but it is mixed with another mood from your spectrum of choices. We didn't kill it because we want fire and anger to be available to us, just as calmness and peace are available to us. What we do learn is that we have choices in the realm of our emotions. We are then able to be more effective in our response to ourselves and to others.

Portal 9
BE AN ISLAND UNTO YOURSELF

"The island (*dīpa*) in Buddha's words is no longer the dwelling-place of a godhead, it rather is identical with Enlightenment, *nibbāna* (*nirvāna* in Sanskrit), the safe ground, or terra firma as Amazonia-specialists say today."
— Author unknown

When he was reaching his eightieth year, the Buddha was instructing his disciples to rely on the island within. When his body was gone and he was no longer there to talk with them, they could still know peace. He said "be an island unto yourself." Rely on yourself. He pointed away from himself and toward the heart and soul of the individual. Go back to what is within you. He instructed an ancient "How to" system of self-reliance. The words of the Buddha are still alive in the writings of his disciples and in the (*dharma*) teachings.

The energy that was in the living Buddha and the living Christ is in each and every one of us. Some are aware of this and others are not. Some see the Buddha and the Christ as men. It doesn't matter how you relate. I find that at times I want to speak to the entity as I would a wise friend; at other times I want to feel their energy in my heart. No matter how you can relate to this idea you will still benefit from this portal.

Think of the Buddha as the embodiment of all the virtues of the great spiritual masters. If you prefer you may use any other one that you wish from your religious or spiritual tradition. Just substitute your deity for the word Buddha.

Practice

Begin by bringing the deity into your presence. See his or her image any way that you wish. It is helpful to begin with an image of a person. Think about the statues or drawings you've seen. Breathe quietly and feel the presence of the great one. Stay with the image for several breaths and feel the closeness. Think of what a conversation would be like with this being. What would you ask? What do you think he/she would say to you? Continue with a conversation for as long as you like.

Slowly and gently allow the image to fade away, but not away *from* you, but rather *toward* you, into your heart. Allow the Buddha to settle in your heart space. All of the attributes, all of the dialogue is now implanted in your heart. You have the energy of the Buddha with you at all times and forever. His spirit is your spirit. When you need to have the living image next to you, bring it back. You are an island of refuge, peace, stability, and contentment.

Portal 10
DO ALL IN THE PRESENCE OF LOVE

This portal is to be done throughout the day. Let love be your guide today. Remember how it felt when you were with your lover or best friend. For today, let love be your best friend and loved one. Let love caress you. Feel it entering through your inhaled breath. Feel its presence in the food as the flavor bursts in your mouth. Taste it in the water you drink. It is not just water; it is an elixir of love. Walk with love today. Love is shining in all the eyes you see. Love is in all of the words spoken. At the heart of everyone you meet today is love. You are always in the presence of love.

Portal 11
YOUR REAL MOTHER AND FATHER

Who are your parents? Of course you will answer Mary and John Smith, in my case Olive and Marshall. But let's take this to another dimension. Not Adam and Eve as many might think, but for now, let's look at our parents in another way as the male and female energy that permeates this universe—that which creates life, and continues the species. There is an underlying "urge to be" programmed into creation. A deeply imbedded desire to make life.

This universal aspect of love must have wanted you to be a part of this creation. You were loved before you were conceived. You were meant to be here. Yes, you came through a particular mother and father, as I did having Olive and Marshall as parents. It is through your parents that you were born. There is a larger, more essential parent whose seed is the seed of all life. The universal energy of creation. The mother and father of all mothers and fathers. We'll think of this energy as the power of love. A power so strong that you must never feel unloved or alone. You are the child of a loving universal energy.

YOGA LESSON: In *Samkhya* philosophy, *Shakti* is the female energy of nature and *Shakta* is the masculine energy of power. Within these two forces is the potential for creation. We are the two in one. Next time you see your parents, know them to be the offspring of the universal couple. Love them just because they were also meant to be here and they come from love. Maybe your parents didn't exhibit this love, but that energy is still what created you. Think about this: the entire universe is a single, unified field of interacting forces. I believe that includes human beings. Now never forget you were born out of the energy of love.

Portal 12
THE BLANKET OF PEACE

This portal is a wonderful way to fall asleep at night, and if you are ill, it will lift your spirit and make you feel better.

Practice

Lying on your back on the floor or in bed, begin to breathe fully, taking in and letting go of the breath in deep sighs. Releasing tension on the out breath. Breathing in nourishment. Using your wonderful power of imagination, notice there is a blanket folded at your feet. It resembles rolled up netting or gauze, which is white and sparkling. It almost looks like a cloud. It is very soft and fluffy. It has a slight movement, like your breath.

Imagine yourself reaching down for the blanket and gently unfolding it over your feet and legs. You feel the aliveness of the blanket and realize it is not just lying on your skin, but it is penetrating into your bones, into the cells and marrow deep within. It is a healing blanket and it sparkles with clear sparkling energy. Pulling it gently upward to your hips you now feel the vibration of healing in your pelvis. You pause and allow the healing energy to move deeply inside your body. (Pause for a longer period of time at any area that needs additional healing.)

Move further up to your navel center and pause to take in the vibration to the center of your belly, into your colon and intestines, your lower back, into the kidneys. Breathe and allow the healing to take place. Moving up to your chest, bring the blanket into position and gently let it fall to your chest and arms. It is healing your spine and ribs, all of your inner organs, the liver, pancreas, stomach. Feel the magic of the blanket healing your heart, removing any emotional pain that abides in the heart. Feel the love pouring into your heart.

Continue to unfold the sparkling gauze until you bring it to your neck and head area, where it gently vibrates the energy into your face, your eyes and mouth, nose and ears, your tongue and throat. Let it heal your brain and your skull. Open your mind to the healing touch of this magic blanket. Feel all the cells of your body receiving this gentle, penetrating energy of health and happiness and deep rest. Stay as long as you like.

When you are ready to put your blanket away, take your time rolling it downward and as you do, notice how you feel. Using your imagination, place it in a special container where it will remain until next time you do this exercise.

Portal 13
YOUR PERSONAL RHYTHM

Place your hands on your belly and breathe. Feel your belly rising and falling as you take 10 deep breaths. Now move your hands over your heart center and breathe, feeling the rhythm of the breath moving the chest. Don't control your breathing. At this point let it be your natural breathing pattern. Pay attention to your breath as it rises to a crest, and falls to relax. See how much it is like the ocean tide flowing in and out. Your breath has its own special rhythm. This is life. It is your own song. Gentle and musical, soothing and calming. Through all of your pleasures and pain there has been the constancy of the breath. Through all of your days the breath is flowing, nourishing and soothing. Pay attention to your own rhythm. Listen closely to the sound. Let all other sounds fade to the background and focus only on your breathing.

Tuning into your breath is just about the easiest meditation you can do. Continue for as long as you wish. Anytime you're in a stressful situation go to your breath. Recently I had a dental appointment that required holding my mouth open for a long time while there was loud and extensive drilling. When my dentist was ready to begin, I focused on my breath and kept my attention there the entire time (about 30 minutes). If something my dentist did intensified the work, I stayed glued to my breath.

Try this next time you undergo a procedure with your doctor or dentist. I think you'll find that your personal rhythm will enable you to get through many stressful situations.

Portal 14
PRATYAHARA
The Tortoise

This portal is about discipline. About being in charge of our senses. When we are having difficulty being disciplined to stay on a diet, practice mediation, or prepare for a test, this meditation will help. If we are not able to concentrate and change our habits, whether it is about eating the wrong foods or sitting to meditate, we need to have discipline. We need to use our willpower. Your Self (with a capital S) must be in charge; otherwise all of your habits, both the good and the bad, will have power over the design of your life. This is the key to happiness and power in your life.

Practice

This is a matter of mind over sense activity. We cannot stop the senses from furthering their function and we wouldn't want to do that. Instead we are going to think of this practice as taking the energy used for feeding the senses and using it for meditation and furthering consciousness. Just for these few minutes, deprive the senses from using the energy. The eyes will not search for something to see, the tongue will not taste, the ears will not hear, the skin will not feel touch or the nose smell. Now imagine all of the energy it took to feed the sense organs being placed at the ajna, the sixth chakra. Slowly, one sense at a time, gather the energy and bring it up to the third eye center just above the eyebrows.

Now that the senses are quiet, with eyes closed, slow and rhythmic breath, hands folded one over the other in your lap, body at rest, hold your attention to the place between the eyebrows and allow your eyes to look upward slightly cross-eyed. Feel like the tortoise withdrawn into itself, energy at the third eye, all else at rest.

YOGA LESSON: Pratyahara is the fifth step of the Ashtanga yoga system. It means detachment or withdrawal, restraining the senses from reaching out for sense objects. The practice of pratyahara is like the tortoise withdrawing its head and limbs into its shell. Each of the parts being withdrawn represents one of the senses being restrained from activity. Practicing withdrawal produces a strong will. Depriving the senses brings about deep stillness within. Repeating this practice strengthens our meditation.

When you have accomplished the technique of sense withdrawal it will feel like you are running a successful business or household, now your private world has a great administrator and happy productive servants—the senses. A sage named Sri Yukteswar counseled his devotees to "Roam in the world as a lion of self control. Don't let the frogs of sense weakness kick you around."

Portal 15
POISED

This is a quick and direct portal. Simply enter the meditation. No analyzing, no talking to thoughts, no direction or reporting to a self, no holding on. Be centerless, no subject or object. Let nothing upset your poise. Remain in the experience. No observer. Poised in pure experience. Walk in and sit. Stop. Just say, "stop." Yes, it can become that easy, just do it—Here and Now.

Portal 16
FORGIVENESS

The *Anahata chakra* is associated with the heart center. It is situated at the center of your chest on the same plane as the physical heart. Here is where we keep our loved ones. Not just as thoughts in the mind, but more than that. I think the heart center remembers the emotion of loving. The bond of love continues unless it is broken by an action that creates a reason for a change. Often that change in feeling creates great sadness and emotional pain and it is almost like our heart is bruised, and in fact, the cliché is that "he broke her heart" (or vice versa). We'll just say it is emotionally bruised.

The Anahata chakra is the center of love. Through it flows the energy connecting us with all of life. When balanced we can give love generously without fear, and we learn to allow ourselves to accept love from another without fear. It is a chance we all take. Sometimes it doesn't work out. Ask yourself if you would give love a chance even though you knew it could result in injury? When the Anahata chakra is balanced we will answer yes.

With the following portal we will explore a way to reestablish harmony and balance to this chakra, and be on our way to healing a broken or bruised heart. There may be other issues involving forgiveness that can also be addressed through this practice.

Practice

Inhale and exhale several times allowing your body to relax. As you exhale, let go of any tension or tightness in the body. Feel the muscles letting go and softening. Move around and stretch if needed and then continue the breathing. Keep the breath moving until you feel that the tension has cleared.

Move your attention to your heart space deep within the chest (in the direction of the rhythmic movement created by your breath). Begin with clearing and cleaning. With each deep breath you take in, feel the life force within the breath re-energizing and purifying the Anahata chakra. Know that it is your choice to hang on to old pain and grudges. Know that you can let go of the hurt you have received. It really is a choice. Just as a physical wound takes time to heal, emotional pain can take even more time. Place your right hand on your heart space. If you begin to feel emotional, ask yourself, why?

And now address the emotion. Look it right in the face. Who do you see? Can you forgive that person? Or is it you who you are angry and upset with? Are you strong enough to say I forgive you? Say to that person or to yourself, I need to move on with my life. I'm letting go of the pain you caused me. Move the healing energy to the person and offer forgiveness by holding your hands in Anjali (prayer) pose. No matter how angry you are, and no matter how bad that person is, until you can forgive it is difficult to create space for another.

On a personal note, when I was first investigating yoga many years ago I attended a class in a woman's home. She offered a meditation at the end of the yoga *asana* practice. So I sat, and before I knew it something had triggered thoughts of my father. He was an alcoholic. He was the funniest, nicest, most loving man when he was sober and none of those when he drank. I didn't realize how much pain I had bundled up and tucked away over the years, but it burst out in tears that evening. I was embarrassed and made an excuse to leave. I realized later that I had not gotten over all the emotional issues surrounding my childhood, and in order to do so, I would have to resolve the problem or I would be crying at every sitting. It took time, but I figured it out. I persisted in sitting and practicing yoga. Each time I would sit I would bring him into my mind. Just recognizing this deep-seated pain was a major step in my healing.

As I continued practicing yoga meditation, I visualized my father and told him (he had long since joined AA and was deceased by now) that I now understood that he had problems that needed addressing, and so did I. I would say to him, "I am sorry for your pain and the pain you caused yourself and your family. May you rest in peace. I forgive you and I love you."

I now felt ready to sit in meditation with a clear mind, knowing that it was a *samskara* "activator" that I had dealt with and resolved. It took more than one sitting to overcome the pain; however with patience and persistence I was soon able to sit and meditate peacefully. It is true that each time we bring a memory to the forefront of our thinking, we tend to make it stronger, but with yoga we "break up" the thought by asking questions and replacing the thought with something positive—for instance when I would think about my father in meditation, I thought of him as the funny, loving man he was and I forgave him for the pain. Forgiveness gave me peace.

 I hope this portal helps you to do the same. It may take time and many sittings, but be patient and gentle with yourself. It is important not to push yourself. If you cannot visualize without becoming very emotional after practicing this portal a few times, it may help to seek counseling. Had I not had the guidance of Gurani Anjali and an understanding of yoga psychology, I probably would have had to seek counseling, or perhaps I would have continued to simply ignore the effects of a difficult situation.

 You are at the center of your feelings of love, and you can now feel the clean, clear, openness of your heart space.

 Let it begin to move outward from your heart center by offering love to all beings and especially those who are in pain.

 Stay relaxed but focused on the experience. All of the love you have held dear to you is enclosing you in its embrace. In your daily life as memories come up, realize that was the past and you are not there now. You are here and now. May you always be able to give and receive love.

Portal 17
A HEALING BATH

This portal brings us to a deep level of relaxation where healing can take place. It is important to practice in a warm room with several blankets nearby to put over you if needed. This is an especially wonderful portal when your joints and muscles are aching.

Practice

Close your eyes and be sensitive to your environment. Now focus on your body and especially your skin and the area right under your skin. Take several deep breaths and feel the heat in your body. Be aware of the heat penetrating your skin and moving slowly into your body. Feel the heat moving beyond the skin and through the tissue and cells to your bones and joints. The warmth is seeping into your entire body. Feel it in your head and jaw and skull. Your shoulders and arms, the joints in your fingers. Breathe deeply and feel your chest move and be filled with warmth. Move to your belly and feel the deep penetrating warmth of the sun entering your intestines. Fill your belly with warmth. Feel the joints in your back and your hips being healed from the heat of the healing bath. Move down your legs and into the joints in your knees and ankles and toes.

Feel the healing and relaxation. Now lie still in full body awareness of the warmth. Relax and enjoy for several more minutes before you slowly move your body.

Portal 18
BE BREATHED

This concept is one that seems to get me out of myself and remind me that I am part of a universe of living and breathing beings. I am one of many.

Practice

You may sit or lie down for this portal. Feel the life in you. Breathe in and know this is the breath of life. It is the closest and most important thing you have. Honor the breath. Exhale and relax. Take a deep breath in and out a few times. Take it in deeply. Now give it back. Exhale and release all the toxic energy you may have encountered today. Release tension and tightness. Breathe in again, letting the universe give you a new and refreshing breath. Continue to breathe in this manner and with each breath be thankful for the gift of life. Take in the breath like a newborn. It is perfectly natural to give the breath back when it's our time to do so. But for now, enjoy and honor the breath flowing through all things including you.

Portal 19
OM

Om is a sacred Sanskrit word that has been chanted daily since early times in the East. In *The Encyclopedic Dictionary of Yoga*, Georg Feuerstein describes it as the "root" or *mula-mantra*. Om symbolizes the Divine. It is the sound of the soundless.

Practice

Om is a very powerful syllable. When chanted during meditation it focuses the mind. Begin by chanting aloud. Inhale a deep breath and open your mouth, listening to the sound you are making as you release the OM. Feel it in your chest, coming up to the mouth, moving across the oval space of your mouth. See the OM physically as if you are making a shape, an oval or a round shape, and release it out of your mouth. Listen to the sound. Watch the shape of OM get smaller and lower in tone until it is gone. See how long you can make it last while keeping your attention on the sound. Follow it all the way to total silence.

Breathe in again and form the word once more. Repeat several times aloud. When you don't feel the necessity to chant aloud any longer, simply let the entire process transfer to your mind and breathe the word silently, still paying close attention to the sound as it begins and slowly fades away.

Stay poised at the end of the word and hold the silence for as long as you can. Repeat chanting aloud anytime your focus begins to fade.

Portal 20
THE END OF THE SENTENCE

You know that space at the end of a sentence right after the period? What is there? Nothing. A hesitation. A pause before the next thought. A full stop. We have so many thoughts going on at the same time. We choose some to dwell on and others fall away without our attention. Like reading or writing, we create a dialogue composed of ideas that we sort out of this mishmash.

Practice
Instead of looking at these thoughts and perhaps picking out what we want, we will let the words run on until we find a place to stop. When you are able to ignore the many thoughts, pick out a sentence from them or make up a sentence out of what is most on your mind—nothing too important. Form this sentence on the "paper" of your mind and put the period or a full stop at the end. Make it really emphatic. It's black and big. Now keep your mind centered right there, and slowly, as you feel you can release it, move to the space next to it. Stay in that space. Enjoy the peace and quiet of a still mind. If you start to venture out of that space, take a breath and return. Practice for at least 10 minutes. If you cannot focus on the space, instead stay with the period at the end of the sentence. Sometimes we just need something more tangible to hold on to.

Portal 21
A MINI-VACATION

Finding the neutral space is a very pleasant meditation; like the prior one it is a visualization that helps us to find the bliss of peace within. Like we are taking a mini-vacation.

Find the neutral space between pleasure and pain. Right now we are not seeking pleasure or avoiding pain. We are neutral, in between events that tend to pull us here and there. We're traveling to a place called "non-duality." Rest here in this place between yourself and the world. The inside and the outside. The "I" and "thou." This is a lovely resort and it's really inexpensive so prepare to stay for awhile. Create a place you can visit whenever you feel pressured from the outside world. Fill your private room with objects of beauty that make you happy and at peace.

Practice

Imagine yourself sitting in a comfortable chair, within your restful private room, gazing out the window. Look at the sky and let your mind rest in the space of the sky. Stay in this quiet, peaceful place and view the sky for as long as you wish.

When you are ready to return from your vacation, slowly come back to the place where you are sitting. Welcome your self with a smile. Welcome the magnificent, magical world around you. See the magic in the world for the rest of the week. Take a vacation once a day. I hope you will be amazed at the peaceful place within, and the beauty of the world. Enjoy the quiet time on your vacation; equally enjoy an awakened view of the world around you.

In "Leaves of Grass" Whitman said: "As to me, I know nothing else but miracles. To me every hour of night and day is a miracle. Every cubic inch of space a miracle."

Can you view the world this way?

Portal 22
SO HAM

The Breath Mantra

The So Ham mantra has been called the universal mantra because of the fact that its vibration is the sound of the breath, and everybody breathes. Soooo is the sound of inhalation, and Hammm exhalation. It is a sound that is with you all the time.

Practice
Close your eyes and focus on your breathing. Inhale and exhale. Relax. Notice thoughts, desires, and emotions. Simply observe. Move mentally away from your thoughts and go to your breath. Observe the breath movement and begin to plant the mantra in the breath. *Sooo* inhale, *Hamm* exhale. Keep repeating the syllables of the So Ham mantra with each breath. Repeat the sound out loud at first until you feel ready to repeat it silently. You are calling to the sound of your breath. After a time you will notice that you are listening rather than saying the sound. Continue to be still and listen until it becomes a song being sung to you. Hold to the sound. You have awakened the mantra that is already there. It is the breath's song. Let it descend upon you like a blessing or benediction.

Throughout the week continue to listen to the breath sound; you do not need a special time or place to sit. All the time you are shopping, cooking, cleaning, working, even conversing with others, the sound is there.

This is the simplest of all mantra meditations. It was given to you the day you were born.

YOGA LESSON: The *So Ham* mantra is also called the *Ham Sa* mantra. *Ham Sa* poses the question, *Who am I?* So Ham provides the answer, *I am that*. I have also seen it as *So Hum*.

It can be confusing, but for our purposes in this portal we will focus on the sound of the breath, rather than interpreting the meaning and pronunciation. Listen and see if you can find the word that fits your sound.

Portal 23
THE LAKE OF THE MIND

The mind's activity is often compared to a lake or a body of water. Yoga is *citta vrittri nirodha*: modifications of the thought waves in the mind. In yoga we learn to recognize the nature of the mind. Knowing the mental activity of the mind, we can modify our thought waves to bring about the desired effect. In a storm the water is affected by the wind, which causes turbulence, from mild ripples to pounding violent wave action. Our mind is affected by the movement of our breath; in fact, the yogis have long taught that the breath is the fly-wheel to the nervous system, and when we are violent or angry our breathing changes into a short, rapid pattern. We can hardly catch our breath. We become hot. The mind is out of control with rage and we say and do things we would not have done if we exercised control. Seeing this, the yogis wisely developed systems of breathing to cool and heat the body, to increase energy, and to calm the mind.

Practice
With this knowledge close your eyes and begin to breathe slow, deep, calming breaths. Bring to mind a body of water; a lake you may have visited or seen in a photograph. Imagine a breeze flowing over the lake and causing ripples on the surface. Focus now on your breath being the wind causing the ripples on the lake and breathe

slowly in order to slow down the movement. Keep breathing and focus on stilling the water. This may take several minutes. Take your time. Hold your mind to the task. When you have stilled the water completely, notice how your mind is as serene as the lake. You have modified your thought waves.

Portal 24
HOLDING AN ORANGE

My Gurani would hold a piece of fruit in her hand. I remember a large brightly colored orange. She would hold it like it was a most precious thing, a great, orange jewel, and ask, what is this? What do you see? You might say "an orange." But what is an orange? What does the word *orange* say about this fruit in her hand? What else can you see?

Thich Nhat Hanh held a paper in his hand and asked the audience, what do you see? He saw the cooperation it took by nature, including man, to make the "paper." It is a revelation to realize what something is besides the word we casually associate with the object. I heard Guruma say many times over the years that "a thing in itself does not exist."

Practice

Get a piece of fruit and place it in front of you on a table. What do you see? Examine the fruit carefully and lovingly. How was it created? Where did it come from? What did it take to "make" this piece of fruit? Do you see the water, sunlight, earth and care in it? What else? Take your time and like a detective, explore the fruit, and consider what you see. Now with complete attention, begin to prepare the fruit to eat and share it with someone you love. Will fruit ever be the same old thing for you?

Portal 25
EXPLORE YOURSELF

There are two parts to this portal. In the first we ask ourselves questions that apply to our personality and habits, and in the second we ask the question "Who am I?" By using inquiry we can get a deeper knowledge of who we are on many levels. I developed a habit many years ago of evaluating my life at the turn of each season. It is autumn as I write this, and I've already done my work, deciding that in addition to completing some of the writing I've been doing, I'll write more poetry. I also recognized the need to establish a more structured time for meditation. If I don't choose an exact time, I start other things. So first thing after a cup of tea I will sit for at least 15 minutes. You may try making this a habit.

I'll give you a few questions just to get you going, but remember for the first part you need to make this personal. When we get to the great question, Who am I? I'll simply advise you to use it as your meditation.

Practice, Part 1

Get a notebook or pen and paper. The first part will be a list of questions taken from my suggestions, or you may personalize them. Take plenty of time doing this, maybe several days. Keep in mind that at different times in our lives, our questions will vary depending on the moment of inquiry, but try to ask the more essential, the deeper, more important questions. Moods change like the wind. Some of my suggestions are these:

Who are the most important people in my life? Am I serving them well? What would I change? If you included yourself in this inquiry that is perfect, as you have to be the starting point and that leads to the next question. Are you happy? Are you content? Is there a facet of your personality you would prefer to change? Are you living up to your highest standards? If not, why not? Is it in your power to change? Do you have choices? Tell yourself what changes you would like to make, and how you can implement them satisfactorily. Write it down.

Take your time and return to this portal often. Pick one question and work with it until you're satisfied. These are explorations into your self. Have a conversation with yourself in order to learn who you are. We may go through life still accepting what may not be serving us any longer. At times you may not be able to answer the question. Or the answer may lead you to another question, as in "Are you happy?" Use these questions as entries into knowing yourself, or make a list of questions that are designed for whatever is going on in your life right now.

The second part of this portal takes the inquiry deeper, going beyond the personality and behavior. It comes from Ramana Maharshi, a great Indian sage who taught around the beginning of the twentieth century. He practiced and taught a method of self-inquiry expressed by the question "Who am I?" He didn't give formal mantras to his followers; rather than using an external approach, he felt that repeating the pronoun "I" brought the seeker closer to the mystery of themselves.

Practice, Part 2

Use the phrase "Who am I?" as your meditation, and see where it takes you. What part of you cannot be dismantled? Can you find that part that is permanent and unchangeable? Maharshi's teachings are considered "the direct path." Begin with sitting in your spot and practicing deep breathing. If you have a place where you meditate and you have set up an altar, light a candle and see the candle as your body, the wick as your mind, and the light of the flame as the essence of your being, the Self. Think about Ramana Maharshi and his instructions for attaining realization of your deepest self. Very simply, in the silence beyond thoughts allowing full relaxation of body and mind, repeat the phrase "Who am I ?" This inquiry will take you beyond the ego.

Portal 26
PEACE MANTRA

Om Shanti

According to Georg Feuerstein, the word *mantra* is derived from the verbal root *man* (to think) and *tra*, suggesting instrumentality. It is a thought or intention expressed as sound.

Om is an example of a sacred sound. Mantras can be one word or many. When a guru gives a mantra to his/her disciple it is usually just one or a few words and is considered a very potent formula for meditation. A mantra can also be a sentence, such as the Gayatri Mantra given in the invocation at the beginning of this book, or it may be something given more casually for health, wealth, and good fortune.

When I received a mantra from Gurani Anjali, it was when she saw that I was experiencing a level of consciousness referred to as *samadhi*. She took a few weeks before the ceremony took place to consider what mantra was the right one for me. She whispered it in my ear and I was not to share it with anyone else.

There are many mantras that are available to everyone, such as the Buddhist *Om Mani Padme Hum*. A Christian may not call *Maranatha* a mantra but it does fit the description. Early Christian monks chanted this word, which means "Come Lord." The intention is the same, a sacred formula used in meditation.

A mantra that is prescribed specifically for a disciple is a unique key to open the doors of consciousness. The Guru knows what the shape of the key is for that individual. Both types of mantra are very powerful when employed with serious intention. Mantra is a special language that speaks to eternity. The Sanskrit language is ancient. It speaks of sages, rishis, and gurus who understood the nature of the spirit and how to speak with it. I don't believe that repeating "one" or "peace" is the same thing, but I do think if they are said with sincerity and devotion, they can be effective.

Practice

Earlier I used *So Ham*, the breath mantra (see Portal 22). Here we'll use the mantra Om Shanti. Sit and watch your thoughts until they slow down. Begin to think about the word *peace*. What does it mean to you? How does it feel to be peaceful? Imagine the people around you at your home or your workplace feeling this way. Imagine neighborhoods interacting in this state of peace. Do you feel happy while in this mood? Now you are both at peace and happy. They seem to go together naturally. Notice the energy level while in this feeling. Does it seem that this state of mind requires very little energy?

The Sanskrit word for peace is *Shanti*, and the mantra begins with *Om*. Begin to say *Om Shanti* either aloud or silently to yourself. Now the peace and happiness is flowing through your whole body, enveloping you in an atmosphere of peace. Move this energy outward to your loved ones wherever they may be. Sit and think of projecting the energy outward to friends, neighbors, and community. Sit and allow the energy to flow outward to all people everywhere. Stay in this circle of peace with all humanity. Now circle the whole Planet Earth in this energy you are emitting. Continue to sit for as long as you wish.

If you would like to feel connected to me and to other yoga practitioners in class on Tuesday night, sit for meditation and join us by chanting *Om* and then *Shanti* three times, "Peace for myself. Peace for my loved ones, my friends, and family wherever they may be, and peace for all beings. May we all know peace." This mantra is similar to one from the Buddhist tradition.

Portal 27
VISHUDDHA CHAKRA

Place the palm of your right hand at your throat center, just at the front of the throat. Make a sound like "mmmmm" and listen and feel the vibration. What you probably will say is that you hear sound (*sabda*). A sound such as "mmmmm" is meaningless, like the sound of rain, or wind. Sound, as we know, is also meaningful and manifests in speech. According to the yogis there is a specific sound connected to each psycho-energetic center (chakra). The throat center is called *jalandhara* (water pipe seat), also referred to as "the pure wheel." Its color is smoky or greyish purple. The mantra or sound for the throat center is *ham* (said like *Om*).

Practice

With your hand at the throat center begin by making any sounds you wish. Test out your equipment by paying attention to all aspects of sound. Make sounds that are meaningful and nonsense. Make sounds that you enjoy hearing and some that you dislike. Grunt and groan, low and high. Try making the sounds of animals, birds, and bees. Investigate the feeling of the sounds in your body. Where do you feel it? How do different kinds of sounds make you feel? Are particular emotions connected to the sound? Take several deep breaths, and feel the sound of your breath.

Now that your throat has your full attention, we can begin the meditation. You may sit in any comfortable position. It is not necessary to keep holding the throat center, but if you become distracted it may help to do so. Bring your full attention to the throat and visualize a smoky, hazy purple color in the form of a full circle. Like the full moon. Take your time forming the circle and developing a color. Keep your attention within this circle and explore the space within the circle. Breathe naturally, but be aware of a sensation at the throat center as you breathe slowly and rhythmically. After several minutes (or as much time as you wish), begin to chant the sound of the *Vishuddha* chakra *Ham* very softly, and keep your attention on the sound. Let it float in the circle of purple. Then let it move toward the center of the circle. Hammmm. Breathing slowly, keep the sound at the center as if it is balanced in the center and your breath keeps it there. Move your attention slowly into the center of the word *ham* within the circle. Go to the center. Go to the space and allow *ham* to envelop you. It is now surrounding you. Relax and enjoy this wonderful experience.

When you have completed the meditation on this portal you will know sacred speech. After the meditation, take the experience with you and move through your day with an awareness of sound (*sabda*). What do you hear? What sounds do you make? Are you saying what you believe to be true? What do you want to make manifest through speech? What will your word create for you?

Portal 28
PATH TO THE HEART OF LOVE

We will walk slowly hand-in-hand
We'll need to travel light
Leave your baggage here
Leave your familiar place and things
Your home, your town, work families friends and
    enemies, your pets
Leave your past and future

Being an astronaut of inner space
We'll need to leave our senses here
The sense of smell and taste and touch
We'll need to leave our usual emotional responses here
Leave your fears, anger, hopes and dreams
And be open to explore whatever arises

Take a deep breath
Again, exhale and inhale
As you breathe deeply, move your awareness to your
    heart center
Place your hand on your heart
Hold to the feelings of love, contentment and peace
You know what that feels like
To love and be loved
Now we enter a relationship with ourselves

Know that you already contain all of the love
You will ever need
It will be with you forever
Focus on this abundance of love
Free from attachment
Be absorbed in this splendor
This love.

Portal 29
APARIGRAHA

Non-possession is extremely difficult. It means to be totally detached from all that we claim as ours. Even to the point of denying our identity. We are left totally naked with this realization. What can we own? Does this frighten you? Let's walk through the idea of this kind of total freedom and see if we can create a portal.

We can't remember the time of our birth, but we came with nothing. A fresh, new entity. There are some people who believe we are born like a clean slate, and there are others who believe we carry our past lives and karma with us. For our purpose we'll go with the clean slate theory. We get to know our place in a family and the world. We learn that there are people who will care for and provide for us.

We've accumulated a tremendous amount of "stuff" since that time. Many of these things have come and gone during our lives. We may become upset when we lose something, a precious object, a person. We also have mental and emotional tendencies, some of which are negative to our lives but we hold on for dear life to it all. When the pain is so bad we let go, we give it up, we surrender. We learn and grow and change. So let's ask ourselves what we're holding on to right now. What do we own? What do we possess? Would we be willing to let go if the need or want arrives? There are times when we may not have a choice and in that case we would suffer and then recover. We may even have a hard time remembering our loss at a later time.

Practice

As we sit for this meditation I'd like you to imagine yourself as innocent and free, saying to yourself I accept myself as I am right now. I love myself as I am right now.

Begin the process of entering the portal by withdrawing from the external world. Follow your breath as you enter the inner kingdom to a place of clarity and peace. Clarity because you are not identified with externals, who you are, what you do, and how you look to others. You are pure consciousness without possessions. We are free in this place of basic needs. Stay in this place of *Aparigraha* for about 15 minutes or as long as you wish. You are clean and just born. When you are finished, place your hands at your heart center and acknowledge this clean, clear, pure self that you are.

Now live your day by reducing your needs. Pass along possessions you do not need anymore. Give things to people who either need or have expressed a desire to own them. You must do this willingly; freely let go of them or you will create pain for yourself later. Eat a bit less this week. Enjoy simple, nourishing foods. Make changes that suit you at this time of your life. Let the *samskaras* dry up, and they will invade your consciousness less and less.

Portal 30
LISTEN WITHOUT NAMING

Have you ever been sitting out in the yard and closed your eyes, sighed, and laid back to relax—did you notice that your sense of hearing becomes more acute? Let's capture that moment now.

Practice

Find a comfortable chair indoors or outdoors. Take several deep breaths and gently close your eyes. Now just wait for a few breaths and focus your attention on your sense of hearing. Allow all the sounds around you to enter into the chamber of hearing. All else will be still except for this one sense perception. Give it your total attention. Begin to listen very carefully and closely to the sounds within your reach. The quieter you are, the better you will be able to hear. Let all of the sounds in at once. Lie back or sit back and let them enter. You must just listen, but without any verbal or mental "naming" of the sounds you are hearing. If you hear a train pass by, try not to mentally say train, or annoying. Just let it be one of the sounds in the enormous body of sound.

If you find yourself naming or expressing an opinion, breathe the thought away and begin to simply listen once again. This exercise is most enriching. It will improve your sense of hearing, as well as your ability to listen really carefully. You will also find that you will be able to isolate just one of the senses for greater sense perception.

YOGA LESSON: *Samskaras* (past conditioning) cause the mind to tell us "I hate trains, I love robin calls, I remember sitting with John hearing a robin." On and on, until you cannot remember where you were. Be alert and relaxed and enjoy this beautiful experience. In this portal we are concentrating on the sense of hearing and taking in what is heard without comment. No back talk here.

Portal 31
SOMETHING PERFECT EXISTS

What is that perfection that just *is*? Prior to a thought or an act we can find that perfection. Perfect stillness. We don't know what to name it. What to call it. We find ourselves knowing it from a place beyond language. All is suspended. It is a pure state of beauty and wholeness that cannot be described. See if you find yourself in that place this week. If you do, hold on by being very still. Be very quiet and let it envelop you with its richness. Sometimes less is more.

There are so many opportunities during the day when we will find ourselves experiencing a state of being that just suddenly is there. See if you can be like a detective and when it comes over you, stop everything and stay with it. This kind of spontaneous meditation is a gift. Take it and be thankful.

Portal 32
BREATHE

The following is a personal meditation that came on a day when I was sitting and following my breath. As I did, the words came to me and I just started to write it down as I experienced it. Prepare yourself to sit and read it when it is very quiet. Concentrate on several breaths before starting and then read and follow the words to see what I saw.

Practice

Breathe
Feel the movement of breath traveling through your nose
Feel your chest moving with the breath
Feel your belly filling with the breath
Let it go by exhaling
Feel the breath spread out to your bones
And blood and organs
Out to the skin
Breathe into your brain
Energize and refresh your mind
Clear your thoughts
And feel the space and openness of your mind
Feel the movement
The swelling rising and opening of all of your cells
All of your pores
Breathe into the marrow in the bones
Breathe into all the places and spaces

Let the breath enter the dark places
The shadows and corners of the mind
The hidden places
The secrets, fears, anxiety and hate
Breathe
And feel these dark places fill with light and energy from your breath
Energize these dark places back with the light of love
Convert all these negative unwanted scars into
Tender open healed places
New to you
Clear to you
Refreshed and energized
Create a new being
Free from obstacles
Sanctified with the holy breath
Now expand your breath to include everyone
In this space and place inside and outside
Animals, birds, flowers, forests and trees, oceans, rivers and worlds
Know that all things breathe
We share the energy of existence
All matter converts back to energy
The energy that sustains all things always existed
And always will
Changing appearance like an actor
Changing costumes to become a frog, a tree, a woman
Can we accept the limited existence of matter
The unlimited existence of pure energy.

Portal 33
DAY OF THE DEAD CELEBRATION:
A TRADITION AND A PORTAL

The Day of the Dead is widely celebrated in Hispanic cultures. In the American culture we call it Halloween, and in the Hispanic culture it is called Dia de los Muertos. For several years now, I've attended this day by visiting our local museum where descendants of the Hispanic community set up altars in honor of their relatives who have passed away. It is a joyous occasion where a local band, dressed in skull and cross-bones, plays high-energy music while visitors stop and chat with families. The families are very willing to tell stories and point out grandparents, parents, aunts and uncles in framed photographs. On the tables you will find the favorite foods of the people; one or more tables may have a package of cigarettes, some have shaped sugar skulls, there are lots of colorful flowers especially marigolds. If you get a chance to attend a Dia de los Muertos celebration you will get a chance to see how the dead are brought to life for this day. It is believed that the beloved deceased comes for the day and dances and celebrates with the living. What a wonderful premise.

A few things come to mind as to how this can be a portal for us. If you have a Halloween party and wear a costume, think of your body as part of your costume. Who are you going as? Pretend to be the person or animal you are portraying, and feel that your body has taken on the persona of that character.

We're renting this time on earth in this body. Celebrate and have fun. Stay happy and healthy and humorous for all your days (one day at a time). Another realization from this celebration is to bring your relatives to an altar and add to it anything that reminds you of that person.

Practice

I bring pictures of my Guru, my mother and mother-in-law, and several other members of the family to the altar. I light a candle (sometimes it is the tall glass candles adorned with pictures of saints that you can purchase in your supermarket), burn incense, and set up a vase of fresh flowers. Bring your friends and family alive in your heart and mind for today, dance and sing and play together. Life goes on in different guises. Enjoy the one you are now. Get to know the freedom of this kind of thinking.

Portal 34
SMILE

Smile today. Smile on purpose, work those smile wrinkles. Decide this morning that you are going to smile all day. Just for the joy of it. In fact, right now think "smile" and bring your face into a smile. Your mouth is turned up at the corners and as soon as you do that, ask yourself, how does it feel? When I do this I immediately feel better, I just can't help it. The act of physically "doing" the smile brings about the emotion and I'm simply happy. Sometimes I just walk along smiling and even though I feel silly sometimes, it makes me happy, and silly is fine too. We can also turn that smile into a good laugh. Laughing is the best way to release stress and tension. It is said that kids laugh about 400 times a day compared to adults at 25 times.

Practice

Just smile. Even when you're in pain, even when someone is mean to you, when you're alone, dealing with anyone, today smile at least once. You'll see how a smile can change your day and others as well as the world. See the humor in life's annoyances. Lighten up and see the cosmic humor. One more person exhibited joy today and that made the world a better place.

Maybe we should make a rule that says each person has to smile or laugh a certain number of times a day. This week decide to smile and laugh every day.

Portal 35
FREEDOM FROM THINKING

For today, our innermost desire is to know unconditional happiness, and to feel joy and bliss. Thoughts often get in the way. There are times when we don't need to think, create new thoughts, or look back to fetch old thoughts. Give yourself a moment of freedom from thinking. We can make this choice. The mind will continue to carry on with what it does best, but you can decide not to pay attention to the thoughts.

To do this, begin by imagining that you are entering a dark room and need to find the lamp. You have a flashlight in your hand, and you begin to move the light around the room, passing all kinds of objects as you search for the lamp. You must keep focused and not get caught up in looking at the beautiful vase, the magnificent plant, or the scary shadow on the wall. You want only to find the lamp and have light. You are required to let go of all other thoughts and objects to find it. There it is.

Practice

Now you can use this same technique for finding unconditional happiness. Sit comfortably, taking several deep and relaxing breaths. With each breath, feel that you are moving away from your thoughts (objects in the room) and that you are focusing on the deep well of bliss at the center of your being. Focus on the breath traveling in and out of the body. See the breath as a white shimmering column of light. Stay with the light and the breath. If any other thoughts (objects) get in your way, bring your attention (flashlight) back to the light. It is restful and peaceful to disengage from thinking. We see that objects and thoughts do not make us happy—we *are* happiness, joy, and bliss. It just takes getting rid of all else to realize it.

Portal 36
BE AN ARTIST

What is an artist? We have all heard of some of the most famous artists, but we also know artists in our community and maybe even in our family. We are painters, writers, dancers, and singers, and either you or your friends probably engage in some kind of art or craft.

In this interpretation of an artist, we are talking about you being the artist of your own life. You already have the talent, you've had it since the day you were born. No one is exempt. When we were children and were still in the state of freedom from self-criticism, creativity was natural. Open the cabinet doors and allow a child to freely grab the pots and pans and within seconds, they are banging them together making music. You can probably recall in your own childhood, or you have watched children when in kindergarten or at home creating things out of paper and crayons, or chalk on the street. What happened to that freedom of expression? We got trained. We were told how to do things. We were told yes you can, and no you can't. Our little bodies and minds were steadily filled with conditioning (*samskaras*) until we were properly shaped for society. We need this conditioning to function within a group, a tribe, a culture, and a nation, but our creativity may be lost in the process.

Practice

This week the work is to get back some creative freedom. Be an artist this week. Play this week. Bang on some pots and pans or a drum that you have lying around. Maybe join a drum circle, if there is one in your area. Make some music just for fun, no other reason. Write a poem about an experience this week. It could be a trip to the supermarket or something that happened on your street. Draw something with crayons or pencil and pen. Maybe a flower or animal's face. Or draw nothing, just sit and doodle. I love to doodle. The pen finds a way if you let it. Bake a cake and decorate it with edible flowers.

Take this idea into any area of your life. One rule that goes along with this freedom is to not judge yourself, and to just have fun. Life is an experiment. Let it fly. Take a photo of what you have created so that you will remember to do this exercise more often.

Portal 37
ASSERTIVENESS AND AGGRESSION

Even the sounds of these words are harsh to me. Even the meaning of assertiveness makes me feel that push and force of emotion connected to it. For me both words are very similar in feeling. I understand the reason behind the need for women to be assertive. It is unfortunate that our choice of behavior for combating problems is often exactly the behavior that caused the problem to exist in the first place. He or she is aggressive, therefore I must also be. What does this sound like? They are coming to get me. Does anyone hear a fight coming on?

Examine these words this week. See if they come up in your daily life. Notice how you feel if someone is aggressive or assertive toward you, and also notice how it feels for you to be assertive or aggressive. How do you respond to these behaviors?

What if we try taking another approach. From the yoga *sutras*, you can choose to use *ahimsa* (non-harming/non-violence) as a force to bring the other party to you, rather than pushing them away. When both parties push away, there is no coming together. If we do get what we want through aggression or assertive behavior, it only feels good for a little while for the party that thinks they have won. But if we resolve a conflict with ahimsa, we may not always win, but we will feel good about how we handled the situation. It is possible that the other will still want to win, and will continue to use aggression, and we can only control our own behavior. What we hope for is a win/win situation, but we don't always get it.

Take note of how these behaviors feel to you. Do you feel good? Have you maintained your peace? Did you show respect for both yourself and the other? Mick Jagger sang, "You don't always get what you want"—you may only "get what you need." I feel at peace when using ahimsa as conflict-resolving behavior. I don't feel at peace when I am aggressive and assertive. How about you?

Portal 38
WINTER SOLSTICE HEALING MEDITATION

This portal is similar to Portal 17, Healing Bath, but this one is more meditation oriented. In this portal we will utilize the *mudra* as a sign of thankfulness. This is a wonderful winter meditation, although it can be used anytime the need arises. For more about *mudras* see the yoga lesson below.

Practice

Find a place in your house where the sunlight is strong, perhaps in front of a south-facing window. Light a candle and sit and let the sunlight sink deeply into your bones. The *mudra* of the sun, *Surya mudra*, will help further attract the sun. With the right palm held upward, bend the ring finger toward the palm and hold with the thumb at the first or second joint. Rest your hands on your knees with the palms facing upward.

Begin to chant *Om Surya Shanti Shanti Shanti* several times until you feel quiet and fully in the moment of sunlight and warmth. You may continue to repeat the mantra for as long as you wish. Remind yourself that you have the sun inside of you. You are made up of sunlight and air, of water and rock. You have everything inside of you that is outside of you. The elements exist in nature and you are a part of nature. You are creating a union between the fire that is inside of you and fire of the sun.

See the golden light of the sun shining and glittering off objects around you. Your skin is a blanket of warmth.

Close your eyes and feel the sun's warmth on the inside of your body. Breathe the sun into your lungs, your blood stream, your heart. Taking deeper breaths, allow the sun to penetrate deeply into your inner organs, more deeply into the bones of your body: arms, legs, and spine. Breathe the sun's rays of energy into any pain, weakness, or disease in your body. Take as much time as you wish. Let the sun warm your eyes, mouth, and brain. Feel the energy bringing vitality to your brain.

Complete this portal by placing your hands in *Anjali mudra* (prayer hands) and saying Namaste to the sun. Or you can chant the *Surya mantra* given above.

YOGA LESSON: The word *mudra* means sign, or seal. According to *The Encyclopedic Dictionary of Yoga*, "These mudras give both enjoyment and liberation. They have great curative and rejuvenating power and also increase the gastric fire." I have used *mudras* as a means to concentrate my intention—using the "sign" physically as a means to "seal" a desire, in this case, thanking the sun. This *mudra* attracts energy from the sun. It is said that it has the power to help anxiety.

Portal 39
UNFOCUSED AWARENESS

There are many times when we need to stay focused. If we were not fully focused on what we are doing during our daily lives, life would be chaos. In meditation we often use the method of fully focusing on a mantra (word or phrase), or a *yantra* such as a geometric form, a candle flame, or our breath. In this portal the method is to be unfocused. We will let life blur for a change. It is expanding and relaxing to let go of isolating our attention to one thing, but it is not the same as simple drifting.

Practice

This is nice to do outside in a quiet place, but indoors at a window will work as well. Take several deep and relaxing breaths, and with each breath let go and relax. With each breath gaze at a single tree or shrub, a rock, or some feature in your vision. Then let go of the focus and very slowly and softly begin to take in more and more of what is in your presence until the picture becomes whole. Whatever occurs in your field is perfect: a bird flies by, insects buzz across your field, a dog runs through and defecates—that's all happening right here, right now. You are part of this field as well; include yourself not as a separate being, not as the observer, the watcher, but as simply a part of this occurrence. Isn't it simply beautiful?

YOGA LESSON: *Yantra* means "device." It is a geometric drawing or shape—the Shri Yantra is perhaps the most recognized. *Yantras* are used for meditation and ceremony.

Portal 40
ANAHATA

Join me
You will take the path that leads to the heart
Anahata is her name
She holds the secret to the true self
You have been brought to the goddess *Anahata*
She sits on a rosy golden throne at the heart center
She is pointing her finger
As we move forward toward her
We see she is pointing at you
She asks that we face ourselves
See yourself in front of you
In the space surrounded by this loving energy
Here there is more love than you ever knew existed
Unite with this energy
Allow all of your cells to open and be filled with love
God and goddess face each other
They walk toward each other and merge into one
You are linked to yourself
Male/female, creator/creation, one/all
Stay and bask in your full and loving self.

After you have enjoyed this merging of consciousness
Take your time coming back to the present moment
Consciousness and creation merge
And bring love to all you touch today

Remember there is a vast unlimited supply of loving
 energy
Just waiting for you to ask.

YOGA LESSON: The *Anahata chakra*, located at the heart, is referred to in the *Yoga Encyclopedia* as "the seat of the Divine." I have held this chakra to be the most sacred and devotional place in my body. When meditating I will place my right hand over my heart and breathe into my chest, with each breath repeating a mantra or the sound of this chakra, *yam*. At times, I will fall asleep repeating the sound, a practice I recommend to you especially if you've had a rough day or you are having trouble falling asleep.

Portal 41
STILL POINT

This is a portal to be used over and over. It was originally created as a three-part workshop to teach meditation. The beauty of it is that it works well for everyone. It is very straightforward.

Practice

Sit in a comfortable position. Your spine should be upright if possible. Wait until your breath is smooth and deep.

Become aware of your body. Stay focused on your body. You are going to make concentric circles from this place where you sit.

Pick a spot in your body. It can be a chakra point such as the third eye center, or the heart center. It can be your belly. Explore your body and find the one that feels right. This is your home base. We will begin at this point and return to it at the end.

Keep your eyes open until instructed differently. Slowly gaze around you, beginning at the home base point. Slowly see the place where you are sitting, the room, the house, look outdoors at the landscape. Take it all in, circling around. Now move further away. Go to the sky, clouds in the sky, birds in flight and as far as you can see.

Now use your imagination to explore the skies, see stars and planets, wild weather, see the Milky Way and our galaxy. Don't try to be accurate, just let your imagination develop the scene. Now bring it all together into a circle with a very small circle in the middle. Stay focused on this image until it is clear to you. Slowly coming back to your body place the image of the circle with the smaller circle at the center, just between your eyebrows and hold it at the *Ajna chakra*. Stay with this image for as long as you wish.

When you are finished with this meditation, slowly open your eyes and know that you are a part of this universe. Regardless of personal problems and national problems, you can find peace in this world.

Portal 42
OVERCOMING UNHAPPINESS

We all have our days. Some days we just get out of bed and a cloud of moodiness covers us. I had one of those mornings recently, but it can happen at any time. We all have ways of dealing with our unhappiness. Some people like to spend time wallowing in the mire of sadness. That's a choice. My gurani used to compare some of this behavior to watching a Grade B movie. Some of the stories we tell ourselves are really quite entertaining. Perhaps for some people this serves some purpose. There are people who have a chronic underlying sadness or unhappiness and are in need of professional advice. That serious condition is not the type of disorder I am addressing here.

YOGA LESSON: In yoga we recognize three primary constituents (*gunas*) of nature (*prakriti*). These gunas are *sattwa*, *rajas*, and *tamas*. The *Yoga Encyclopedia* says, "The power of sattwa enslaves the happy. The power of rajas enslaves the doers. The power of tamas enslaves the deluded and darkens their judgment."

Rajas is a dynamic principle. It has the nature of seeking pleasure, attraction, and clinging to action. It is excitable, lustful, and passionate. In our present-day culture, it is the constant need for stimulation. The question is whether you are enslaved by it. Do you need constant stimulation?

Sattwa (sometimes *Sattva*) is beingness. This *guna* has the qualities of lucidity, illumination, and purity. In its negative aspect, it can enslave the happy.

Tamas is inertia. When it takes over we feel despondent, sad, and lazy. It "darkens our judgment."

With a greater understanding of the *gunas* we can learn to recognize when the balance in our personal life has tipped to the negative side (as indicated above). In order to attain balance and cultivate the *sattwa guna*, we do yoga and especially meditation, thereby illuminating the mind. When balanced, we are not craving excitement and we are not lethargic. The practice of yoga brings about balance. When we recognize the power that we possess to overcome nature, we are well on our way to happiness.

I have introduced the gunas into this portal because I think we can apply it here, even though the gunas have far greater implications in yoga philosophy. I would say that this morning Tamas was sitting on my left shoulder, whispering sad and lonely songs in my ear. I had tea and watched the birds at the feeder on this cold, windy morning. Feeling moody, I got in the shower. My mind was now on the comforting warmth of the water flowing over my body. It felt good. I let the warm water soothe my body, took a deep breath and closed my eyes. In that moment I felt pleasure (*rajas*). I let go of the darkness (*tamas*) and let in a bit of light (*sattwa*).

There was no conserving water for me this morning. I let it run. I said thank you aloud. Thank you. Thank you to the water. Thank you to the warmth. Thank you water flowing freely and clean. Thank you water for your healing grace. Thank you water for sustaining us. Thank you water flowing in all the rivers and oceans and little creeks and ponds. Thank you for being inside of me nourishing my life. Thank you. May we all appreciate water. We literally owe our lives to water.

What happened? One minute I am unhappy; one shower later I am in bliss, standing in my shower. With one moment of spontaneous appreciation, I changed the world. I changed so the world changed. We are connected to all things. I connected with the element water. I was emotionally healed. In sincerely thanking the water, I moved from unhappiness to happiness, from darkness to light.

When was the last time you thanked the water you wash with, the ice in your drink, the flow of the rain? Next time you experience the invasion of the *guna tamas*, try saying thank you. It can change your world.

Portal 43
CLOUDLESS SKY

Sit near a window where you can look at the sky. The sky is so immense. Where does it begin and where does it end? The horizon is not the sky. It has no edge or final ending line. Beyond what we see as clouds and color it goes on forever. We can't put a stop to it. We can't find a thing in it that stays put. Nothing is stationary. Not like the earth where there is always a guidepost that we say is permanent. Even the huge tree that we see constantly moving with the wind and the seasons, is rooted. Even the tiniest thing has its spot and we expect it to be there when we return. Many things are rooted for an entire lifetime of a human. To our eyes they never change, even though we know they do. Not the sky. It is constantly different. The space beyond the clouds and color blue is infinite.

Spend some time meditating upon the sky and beyond to that infinite space.

Practice

Begin by looking at the sky. Go to a window or outdoors and gaze. Find a pleasant place to sit and enjoy watching for a few minutes. Breathe slowly until you feel calm. Notice how your mind has become calmer and you are thinking less. Now think of your mind looking like the sky and space, as together they come and go, changing form, changing movement from still, slow-moving forms to streaky and fast-moving. Our thoughts are like that. Sometimes calm and smooth and pleasant, other times violent, edgy, fast, and furiously moving across the background of space. Thoughts are changing all the time, but we have learned by now that we can slow down and eventually ignore our thoughts and go to a calm, pleasant place in our minds.

Now you are ready to move inward. Close your eyes and visualize the sky inside of you. Let your thoughts calm down and see infinite space. If thoughts come just let them pass through without giving them your attention (just like clouds floating by). Stay focused on the wide, empty, calming space you've created. If thoughts intrude, watch them, turn the thoughts into clouds and watch them dissolve into vapor. Continue to breathe and watch. Your mind is as infinite as space. The mind is clear and calm. Sit for as long as you wish, holding to the calm, peaceful weather of your mind.

YOGA LESSON: Thinking is part of being human. Here we are reducing the activity. Remember that an important goal in yoga is *citta vrittri nirodha*—modification or cessation of the thought waves in the mind. Think of how it was when you were in school, or any time when you needed to have all of your mental abilities applied to one thing. Notice how when you were doing a task that required your full attention or participation, all other thoughts seemed to have disappeared. In order to accomplish anything we have to discipline the mind.

Portal 44
CROSS BREATHING

This portal is very relaxing. It is composed of two types of yoga breathing (*pranayama*). The first breath, or vertical breath, is called *ujjayi* and we will envision it running up and down the central canal of your spine. The cross breath is called *nadi shodhana* (purifying) or alternate nostril breathing and it will run horizontally from the right brain to the left brain. This breath is sometimes called balanced breathing. This *pranayama* exercise is more than an actual portal, because it is excellent to use when you are in need of calming and quieting. It is also very effective to do before meditation. Before beginning the practice read the Yoga Lesson for translations and descriptions of the exercise and benefits.

Practice

If at any time you feel dizzy or light-headed, stop the exercise and relax, returning to your baseline (normal) breathing pattern. Sit in a comfortable place. Relax and take several deep breaths to bring you to a quiet place. Begin with the *ujjayi* breath. Slightly drop your chin to your throat and tighten the glottis (vocal chords or folds) by constricting the throat. Begin breathing through the nose and feel and hear the breath pass the back of your throat. The sound is similar to the soft snore that can often be heard just before we doze off to sleep. Or it sounds a bit like Darth Vader in Star Wars. Concentrate on the sound as you slowly inhale down the spine, filling the central canal with a soft, relaxing expansion of light and air. Pause briefly. Slowly exhale and feel the breath rising upward, bringing the light and air to the brain and top of your head. Repeat 5 times, increase to 7 as you get accustomed to the breathing. Increase as you wish as long as you feel comfortable. That is the vertical breath.

Now after sitting and returning to your baseline breathing (for as long as you wish) we will go to the horizontal or balancing breath. For this exercise you will use your right hand. (If it is necessary, use the left hand.) You will be using your fingers to control the movement of the breath from one nostril to the other. There are two finger positions that you can choose from. The first one is the traditional yoga *mudra* and the second one is easier for some. Hold the palm of your hand open and up, fold the index and middle finger toward the palm. Your thumb will cover the right nostril when you close off the breath, and the little finger and ring finger will close off the left nostril. Another way of holding the fingers is to place the index finger on your forehead just above the center of your eyebrows, above your nose. Use your thumb to close the right nostril and the middle finger for the left nostril. Try them both and decide which one you prefer to use.

Take your time, it will feel odd at first, until you get used to the finger positions and the rhythm. There should be no stress or force used while breathing. Once you've established the hand position you will do the following:

Place your left (or right) hand on your thigh with the palm facing upward. Position your right-hand fingers and bring your hand up to your nose. Take a soft deep breath in and exhale. Hold the left side of your nose closed with your fingers, and inhale through the right nostril. Breathe slowly but fully. When you are first learning, don't hold the breath very long. Remember there should be no straining or force. Now cover the right nostril with the thumb, hold the breath briefly and open the fingers to exhale out of the left nostril. Now you will return. Inhale into the left nostril (the one you just exhaled out of). Close with fingers. Pause briefly and exhale out of the right nostril. Continue by inhaling right, exhaling left. Repeat for 5 breaths to begin with. Once established, you may do more repetitions.

YOGA LESSON: The first *pranayama* (*ujjayi*) means victorious. I find that *ujjayi* increases the length and fullness of my breath more than any other *pranayama*. I like to think it increases my life force and extends my life. That's where "victorious" comes in for me. Strictly speaking this *pranayama* should be started with the left (*ida*) nostril at night and the right (*pingala*) during the day. In yoga physiology the left nostril is thought to be the moon or cooling nostril and the right is the sun, the heating nostril. The *nadis* are conduits or channels through which the life force circulates. They remind me of a vast electrical system, similar to the ones used by acupuncturists. The main system runs along the spinal column *sushumna* and crosses along the lines of the *chakras* and terminates at the nostrils.

These breathing techniques are safe and very effective. For this portal I have combined the two. Some of the more advanced *pranayamas* require preliminary purification before starting, but *ujjayi* and *nadi shodhana* (purifying) are safe in this practice.

Portal 45
TRANSFIXED

Today I stand at the window in my kitchen. It looks out into a garden where there are bird feeders, a hummingbird feeder and a birdbath. I suddenly find myself caught in the view not as a separate thing but as part of it all. I have blended into the landscape and stand transfixed. No mantras, no words—just steadiness. There is a spontaneous appreciation of a scene and suddenly I am in it so completely that there is no line between my body and all that I observe.

There is a sharpened sense of awareness. The world and I are in perfect rhythm. My mind and body are perfectly still. I am aware of what is happening after a few minutes but I hold my mind in a still, peaceful place. I don't allow my mind to wander. I know I can hold on to it by maintaining the focus and the very smooth, slow breathing that I find myself participating in. Body and mind are fixed and quiet and steady. It is blissful. It is a very unified focus.

Practice

The way to practice this is not to practice, but to be ready when you receive the gift. This is the simplest portal yet. It is given to you. By sharing my experience with you, it may be that you will recognize this experience more easily and know how to remain with it.

Portal 46
ONE WITH ALL

Today is the day I am conscious of my life and the life of all of nature. Begin wherever you are.

Practice

Note: Read this the day before you intend to practice it.

This portal does not require a formal sitting meditation, but you'll need to keep bringing your attention back to the present moment. Set your intention for the day as soon as you get up in the morning. Say to yourself, I know I am part of nature. I am alive at the same time as these trees, plants, birds, animals, and people. We are all breathing. There is a breaking down, and building up going on in each of us, all of us. I am going to connect today on a very conscious level with all that is part of my existence. Whatever I can see, smell, touch with my senses are my family and friends.

Just repeating this to yourself during the day will keep you aware. See the trees as breathing bodies. The tree body is different in many ways from ours, but it is the same in that it has a beginning and an end. Today the focus is aliveness, breathing, living together. Look at the plants and pay attention to how they live and breathe. Pay attention to all that you live with today. No other moment will be like this one.

At the end of the day when you're going to sleep, think of all the lives you connected with today. Send out a blessing to each of them. By doing this portal you will better understand what it means to be part of nature.

Portal 47
FEAR AND DEPRESSION

During a phone conversation with a friend today, she told me that she and her husband had been planning a camping trip when a very unsettling event occurred. She had gone out to the camper and almost immediately felt a deep depression, so much so that she had to get out of the camper. She compared the feeling to being held captive in a room and she just had to escape. As we spoke, we talked about how odd it was since she had enjoyed camping for most of her life. My husband and I have spent many a vacation camping with them, and we had a great time. So what was going on here?

Maybe this has happened to you. For no apparent reason a certain place will have a deep negative effect on you. As yoga practitioners we would try to find the reason behind the experience. What caused the fear and depression?

Several years ago my friend lived where I now live but her children and grandchildren lived in another state. At least once a year she would get in the camper and drive several days to visit with them. I noticed each time that she would return sad and depressed, to the point of tears. Now we chatted over the phone about what it was that had happened in that camper. She realized that these previous experiences were probably the basis for her current depression. When she stepped into that camper the *samskaras* planted in the past jumped up to the present, almost as if she had left something physical in the camper to remind her.

What to do about it, now that she knows? How can she change that *samskara*? The plan we discussed is to recondition herself to the camping experience. I suggested a purification ceremony, perhaps the burning of sage, which has been used since ancient times for purification after a negative experience. As she purifies the camper she will state her intention. In this instance she will name her fears and state that they are based on the past and have no power over her now. Her depression is impotent now. She will be returning to her home and her family each time she ventures out for a camping experience.

Next, we leave those thoughts behind and focus on the new experience she will have in the camper. These new thoughts will be cemented by saying and writing down some of the things she would like to do. I also suggested leaving a physical reminder of this ceremony in the camper. Since she is an artist, this could be an opportunity to sit and paint in the camper, perhaps beginning with just a few minutes and extending the sitting for as long as it is comfortable. Her art may tell her a little more about this experience.

Practice

If you find yourself having an emotional experience and you're not sure why or where it is coming from, use these techniques to understand and to change the *samskara*. I do not wish to imply that it is a simple, one-time process. There are *samskaras* that can take years to diminish. In this case, you repeat the process until they no longer have a grip on you. Imagine a wrestler trying to get his opponent to release his hold—he is working with technique and strength and he just keeps at it until he (or she) no longer has the strength to sustain the hold. Little by little you gain—the *samskara* loses.

Portal 48
WINDOWS OF THE SOUL

Have you ever tried to look into another person's eyes for more than a few seconds? Maybe you noticed, as I have, that it is very difficult. I've thought about why that is and if you know me by now from reading *Portals*, I didn't stop there. To me the experience is so overwhelming, it is like falling into that other person. After a few seconds I feel speechless.

There seems to be a silent witness in the other and I feel it is like our souls are gazing at each other. They say the eyes are the windows to the soul.

I'm not suggesting that we stare into their eyes, but I do think that it is important to see the other, a person in a restaurant who is waiting on us, or a clerk in the market, or our children and loved ones. We seem to try to not make a connection with others and I think it is because we want to ignore them. We don't want to recognize them or we will know we are one, we are each other, and we have to care for that person. We have to see them as we see ourselves and therefore treat them as we want to be treated.

In the book *The Little Prince* by Antoine de Saint-Exupery the fox tells the little prince that if he cares for him he will tame him and then they will be friends. Maybe when we really "see" into the other and have this realization of oneness we have been tamed.

We see the human potential for love. It isn't a matter of looking at a person—this portal is to "see into" to "fall into" the other.

Practice

This week observe the others. Make an effort to look into their eyes just a little longer than you usually do.

Portal 49
WAKE UP AND CELEBRATE

The minute you open your eyes this morning get ready for a party. Get ready to celebrate the day. It's (pick the day) Monday's birthday. Can you feel the excitement? Today, all day, keep your attention on this happy occasion. Fix a special breakfast and sit with this time of day. If the weather permits, eat your meal outdoors. Take a deep breath and smell the day. Reach out your arms and absorb the atmosphere. This is Monday's day and you are invited to be at the party. Know that you are moving with the day and it is a glorious event.

Practice

Pick any day to do this portal and then ask yourself why you don't live each day like this. My Gurani used to say, "Live one day at a time." She meant really live it. Be conscious of what is happening and what you are doing—what your role is—and then celebrate this one day. Don't look forward or back—be in this moment.

Portal 50
SING THIS SONG

I suppose this could be called a very old traditional chant—I know my mother used to sing it as she cleaned house. According to Wikipedia it is an English language nursery rhyme, first printed in 1852. I haven't been able to find the author's name so perhaps it is unknown. The song has been used as a spiritual theme and when I first gave it to my students as a portal and a *sadhana* I wasn't aware of it being anything other than a fun song my mother sang. One day as I was singing it, I realized the deeper significance of the words. I have no idea what the author had in mind. The words that we will use are the chorus:

Row row row your boat
Gently down the stream
Merrily merrily merrily
Life is but a dream

Practice
When you first read these words, sing them a few times. During the week when you'll make them your portal, say the words at first a couple of times. And then think about how I see this song as a portal:

Row row row your boat – Keep moving your body. Take good care of yourself by making sure that you eat well, sleep enough, and keep on exercising, making sure that each day you walk starting with 10 minutes and making it to 30 minutes if you can. Adjust according to your physical condition. Maybe you can only walk 5 minutes and increase to 15. Maybe you can't walk; there are plenty of other parts to move, like your shoulders and arms and your feet and ankles. Move something. Do what you can.

Gently down the stream – Be gentle in your life. We move through the river of time. Ask yourself how you want to "move." Practice *ahimsa* by being nonviolent, seeing that you do not harm anyone, including with your thoughts or words. Think before you speak and act. Touch everything lightly.

Merrily merrily merrily – Don't worry, be happy. Notice that when you are chanting this happy song you feel better, and when you feel better so do those around you.

Life is but a dream – All things come and go. It is here one moment and gone the next. We can barely remember what happened this morning—all the more reason to enjoy and to care and to appreciate our lives.

When you are feeling low or gloomy, try singing these few lines. When you are feeling negative and want to turn positive, sing these words. Think about how you would interpret these lines.

Portal 51
SITTING

Do we ever really experience the act of sitting? We are usually sitting to do something like watching TV, reading a book, eating chips and salsa, meditating. Or are we waiting for something or someone, maybe in the doctor's office, or at the train station. Waiting for the movie to begin, waiting for food to be served. For today we will experience the art of sitting.

Lower your heavy body to the couch. It takes your weight nicely into the cushions. After a deep breath you remember sitting so many times on so many couches and chairs, on the green grass, the cold rock. It's easy. It's what you've done a million times without consciousness being involved. Today is different. We will practice the art of sitting. I'd like you to move slowly and very consciously for this portal. This portal can be done with other common everyday activities like walking, lying in bed, standing in line, or driving the car.

It's a question of being present with a practice we are already doing many times each and every day.

Practice

Begin by choosing where you will sit and pick a chair, preferably a straight chair. Carefully lower yourself on to the seat as you have done thousands of times, but this time move very slowly, concentrating on every move your body makes. Chair pose is a yoga *asana* (*Utkatasana*).

Portal 52
GURU PURNIMA
Honoring Your Teachers

I woke up at 3 o'clock in the morning on July 22, 2013 and noticed that it was very bright in the house. I got up to look out the window to see a beautiful full moon and remembered that today is Guru Purnima, a time when Hindus and Buddhists honor their Gurus. It is always celebrated at the full moon in July. In India it would be the full moon (*purnima*) of the month of Ashada (July/August).

In the Ashram where I received my yoga training we honored all the great spiritual teachers of the past and present, especially our teacher Gurani Anjali. We would decorate the Ashram with pictures or sayings of spiritual leaders. Included might be Vyasa, the Christ, the Buddha, and Mohammed. Candles would be lit and a guided meditation would be given, followed by chanting and singing.

When I was very young I had an altar in my bedroom. Since I was brought up Catholic there was a holy picture, and I always had some kind of flower or leaf, and a special object like a rock that I might have found. I loved having an altar and I prayed and made requests as I knelt before it. Then after many years of not participating in any religion, and making yoga my way of life, I met Gurani Anjali and she introduced the *havan*, an altar much like I had as a little kid. Once again I had an altar in my home and still do. As I look now I see a carved metal table with a photo of my Gurani, a pretty candle, several incense varieties, many gifts from my yoga students, green and gold glass bangles that belonged to Gurani Anjali, and a statue of Siva, the Lord of the Dance. For Guru Purnima I'll add photos of people who have inspired me.

Practice

We are built and shaped by all the people in our lives who have influenced us as we grow into complete human beings. Not a single entity has remained just as they were at birth. We are our mothers and fathers, plus our teachers, relatives, friends, and siblings. Even the most casual of meetings can have a strong effect on one's life. For this portal you'll do the same as I have done for Guru Purnima. I honor Gurani Anjali, the woman who changed my life by teaching me the ancient science and philosophy of yoga, including the principles of Yama (abstinences) and Niyama (observances). She mostly taught by her own example. I'm thankful for her guidance and friendship.

I also honor Mervine, a sculptress I met in my late teens. She took me to galleries, gave me brushes and paper, and encouraged me to draw and paint. She told me I was good at it. Her influence led me to a love of art and gave me the confidence to try new things.

Then there was my Aunt Dorothy, a dancer. She took my sister and me to the ballet and theatre when we were very young. I aspired to be like her and wanted to be a dancer; I went on to love practicing and teaching yoga poses. Then there's my mother, a woman who raised a family as a single mom at a time when that was very difficult to do. She did her best to support my interests and desires. I learned to overcome adversity.

So there are many teachers in our lives, and this is a day to say thank you to all of them. It doesn't have to be Guru Purnima for you to be thankful, but I do suggest that you mark your calendar for this holiday and get in the habit of thanking those who assisted in your development. This way it becomes very special. If that person is still living, visit with them or call them on the telephone. I remember calling Mervine when she was in her late eighties and was in an assisted living center in Texas. I told her how much she meant to me. I'm pretty sure I made her day.

If you are part of a religious tradition, honor the founder of that religion. Bring flowers and a candle to your special meditation place. Bring pictures of the people you are remembering. When you have completed your altar for this day, sit for meditation. Allow the breath to flow into the *Anahata,* heart chakra, and let the waves of thankfulness build while you slowly chant Om Shanti, bringing peace to all of your teachers. Continue to join your energy to the energy of the people you are honoring today whether they are living or not. Einstein said,

"Energy cannot be created or destroyed, it can only be changed from one form to another." This breath flowing in and out of your body represents the interconnectedness of each individual. We are not alone. We are not separate. Give the best of yourself.

I hope that you enjoy this Guru Purnima as much as I have and if any of the other portals I have written become extra special for you, perhaps I will benefit from having had a positive influence on your life.

YOGA LESSON: The Sanskrit word *Guru* can be translated in two parts. *Gu* means darkness or ignorance, and *Ru* denotes the remover of that darkness. *Gurani* is the feminine.

www.ingramcontent.com/pod-product-compliance
Lightning Source LLC
Chambersburg PA
CBHW060158050426
42446CB00013B/2884